Bandana Acres
Rascal's Trip

Think ahead!

Kathy Perry

CHICKADEE
WORDS

Bandana Acres
Acres
Rascal's Trip

Kathy J Perry

CHICKADEE
WORDS

To receive updates on future books in the series, visit Chickadeewords.com

Library of Congress Control Number 2018900669

Hardback ISBN: 978-0-9981291-1-2
Soft back ISBN: 978-0-9981291-8-1
E-book ISBN: 978-0-9981291-4-3

Lexile® Level: 470L
Word count: 2447

Edited by Beth Bruno
Character Design by Mark Baral
Cover & Interior Design by Rachel Lawston

This book is dedicated to all children with a love for animals and who are learning to read. May you always remember that every decision has a consequence – so, think and make decisions wisely!

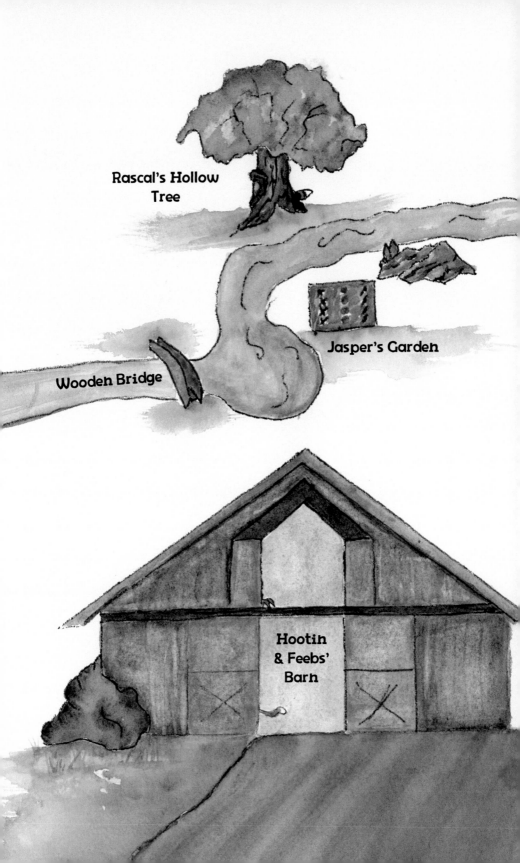

The Storm

Exploring the ravine near his home was Rascal's favorite thing to do. In the creek at the bottom of it he discovered some crayfish and one small silver fish to eat. Water swirled around the rocks along its banks. He should go home, but he wanted to explore just one more minute – or two – or three. **Nothing bad will happen.** He hiked farther away to see what he could find. Small mice scurried under bushy plants. Birds flew to their nests in the trees. But did he go home? No!

The air feels stuffy and warm. He wandered still farther. Then, wind whisked away the stuffiness. The sky filled with dark, ominous clouds that hid the late, afternoon sun. The fresh smell of rain filled the air – and Rascal's nose. Though young, Rascal was old enough to know when a storm was brewing. He waited until it started to rain, and then he turned to race back home.

He ran as fast as he could. A fierce wind blew new green leaves off the trees! It bent the flower heads over. It blew and blew! Nothing could stop it except the rocks of the ravine. Big trees creaked and groaned as if in pain. **CRACK!** Lightning struck a tree nearby. Rolling thunder followed. BOOM! Boom, boom, boom!

"Stop!" he screamed at the storm. But it didn't. "OH!" A whirlwind scooped him up off the ground and took him for the ride of his life!

The Landing

Rascal spun around and around, bumping into broken bits of trees in the swirling wind. He closed his eyes. He curled his legs up. He covered his face with his paws. The wind screamed and whistled around him. He covered his ears to block out the noise.

Then, the wind dropped him. Soft needles and sturdy branches of a tall pine tree hugged him. Dazed, he looked around. His eyes were as wide as saucers, taking in his surroundings.

Rascal cried out loud as he tried to move. "Ouch! My leg really hurts!" It wasn't bleeding,

but it hurt to lean on it. He wished he were safe at home. But first, he needed to get out of the tree. He looked around and worried. *I don't want big eagles or hawks to find me!*

He started down, but sharp pain shot up his sore leg as his weight pushed into it. "Ouch!" he cried again. He turned around to go down backwards. He eased himself down. At last, he was on the ground.

Alone and scared, the little raccoon wondered how far away he was from his hollow-tree home. He had never been so far and felt very much alone in the world.

"I'd better hide," he said out loud. The storm had passed, and night was near. He decided to search the woods for a hole somewhere and found nothing except some small snake holes. *Maybe the rocks up on the hillside would be a good place to hide,* he thought. *I don't want coyotes to find me either!*

Soon, Rascal did find a hole to hide in. Nearly covered by grasses near a tree was a small one.

To make room for himself, he dug some dirt out of it with his good paw and then crawled in to rest. He backed in as far as he could and discovered that it didn't just end; it kept right on going inside the hill. This is strange. Maybe I am in a tunnel, Rascal thought, sighing deeply. I guess I'll explore it tomorrow.

Rascal decided he was safe, for now. His eyelids were heavy. He closed them and fell asleep.

Meet Jasper

Early the next morning, Rascal heard a rustling sound. He opened his eyes, squinting until they adjusted to the sunlight outside. He stretched and yawned. His bad leg felt a little better today.

Then, he heard someone coming!

A rabbit appeared in front of him. He was carrying a bundle filled with fresh foods: lettuce, carrots, and some ripe blueberries. "I heard you come into my house last night after the storm. I slept in the tunnel behind you. Since you blocked the front door, I came 'round from the back this morning. I sure am glad you're not a wolverine! Are you hungry?"

"Yes, thank you," answered Rascal as he came out of the burrow. He chose the juicy blueberries to eat for breakfast. "I'm sorry I invaded your house. I just needed someplace to hide and rest. My name is Rascal. What's that orange thing around your neck?"

"Oh, this?" the rabbit asked, looking over his shoulder at his bandana. "I got this because I share the food I grow with the other bandana buddies. How did you get here?"

Rascal munched on the sweet blueberries and explained how the giant whirlwind had swept him away. "I really need to get home." His voice cracked and his brown eyes filled with tears.

Jasper's eyes met Rascal's. "You've been really brave, Rascal. Jasper's my name. If you need directions around the Big Woods, good 'ole Ollie, the farm dog, can help you. He's a great friend to everyone and really knows his way around."

"A dog? Is he mean like a coyote?" Rascal asked with concern.

"Oh, no. He's very friendly. He wouldn't hurt you at all," answered Jasper.

"Thank goodness," Rascal said. "When can I meet him?"

"We can leave right now. It's not far." Jasper spun around on his heels. He bounded for the farmhouse. Rascal had never seen anyone jump so far and so fast! Poor Rascal couldn't keep up and fell behind. Jasper hopped over the top of the next hill while Rascal slowed to a walk and finally stopped. *I sure hope this path leads to Ollie.* He was frustrated as he watched Jasper's tail disappear over the hill. His injured leg ached from running.

A few minutes later the rabbit returned. "I'm sorry, Rascal. I forgot that you can't run as fast as I can." Jasper tapped his foot as he thought and said, "It'll be quicker if I go alone and bring Ollie back. You wait here for us. I'll be back in a jiffy." Jasper sprinted up and over the hill and was gone.

Boy, he's fast! Rascal sat and rubbed his leg and sighed. In a short time, he was bored. Grasshoppers crawled up long stems of grass and then hopped off to others. Yellow butterflies hovered over purple coneflowers to sip their sweet nectar with long, curly tongues. Birds chirped to each other in the tree canopy above. As the wind wafted over him, Rascal smelled something familiar – something fishy. *I think I'll explore a little bit. I smell food and I'm still hungry.*

Big Water

He took a few steps before he remembered Jasper's instructions to stay where he was. Rascal stopped. He tried to wait, but he decided he just couldn't! *I'll explore a bit and then come right back.* He followed his nose up a steep, wooded hillside and left the path behind him. *I'll remember how to get back,* he reasoned. Later, he rested a bit and looked around at the moss-covered rocks that poked up from the ground."

Rascal sniffed the air. *I think I'm getting close.* He stood up and walked again. The sun warmed the moist air as he got near the ridge.

Once there, he looked down the other side of the hill and saw…water. Lots of it. He hobbled with excitement down the steep hill.

First, he washed his paws. Then, he enjoyed long, cool drinks from the clear water. Rascal explored the shallows for food. He stood on smooth, oval river rocks. The water felt so good on his feet. He peered into the murky water at the pond's edge. A tadpole among the rocks wiggled by. He quickly caught and ate it. But he was still hungry.

A little fish was just a few feet away. He tried to sneak up on it, but the fish saw him and kept his distance in deeper water. Rascal decided to wander a little deeper toward the fish, until only his head was above water. His feet barely touched the slippery rocks below. With his eye on Rascal, the fish quickly swam still farther away. Rascal had to stand on tip-toes to keep his head above the water. But, as he turned to go back, he lost his footing! He tried to swim back. All he could do was beat his good arm and legs against the water enough to stay afloat. Then, he tired, and slipped under the water! Every few seconds he was able to come up to the surface for air. *I've got to get out of this deep water! But how? Oh, why didn't I wait for Jasper & Ollie?*

Ollie to the Rescue

All of a sudden, a big animal swam right under Rascal and pushed him clear out of the water! Rascal was scared, but he clung to the back of the animal as it swam across the pond to the bank on the other side.

"Whew! That was close!" Ollie, the farm dog, glanced across the pond at Jasper, who was standing on a big rock near the edge.

"Everything okay, Ollie?" the rabbit shouted from the bank on the other side.

"Yes, Jasper. Rascal's a little frightened and worn out, but we're both fine. You can go on home. I'll help him home from here. Thanks for coming to get me," Ollie shouted.

"No way! You're not leaving me out of this adventure, Ollie. I'll circle around and meet you on the other side. I'll cross the wooden bridge." Jasper flashed his white, fluffy tail as he turned and jumped through the brush.

"Why didn't you wait for us, Rascal?" Ollie asked. "We didn't know where to find you! Fortunately, I guessed you might come here."

"I tried to. But I was hungry and smelled fish. I was going to come right back." Rascal sighed. "I know now that I should have waited. I'm sorry. I sure am glad you were there for me. Thank you."

"You're welcome. I'm Ollie. Jasper told me what happened to you last night. Haven't you experienced enough adventure? Did you think you could swim with an injured leg?" Ollie asked.

Rascal looked down, embarrassed. "I didn't think about that. I should have thought ahead." He looked up at Ollie's wise face.

"Yes, thinking ahead is very important! Good or bad comes from every decision you make, Rascal," Ollie explained.

Ollie is so wise. "Jasper said you know where my home is. Do you?"

"Well, it's been a while since I've hiked this way, but I think it's over this hill."

"Oh, good! Can we go now? I feel fine." Rascal was excited.

"Sure, let's go." They turned to go up the hill and followed a path through Big Woods.

Home At Last

Rascal followed Ollie closely as they traveled through the dense forest. They climbed over many branches broken by the storm. The little raccoon liked the way the dog really cared about him. He trusted him.

"It sure is a mess out here, isn't it?" Ollie asked. "The hollow tree I remember isn't far from the other side of the next ridge. I used to wander this way, but I haven't for months."

Even though he was anxious to get home, Rascal started to relax. "Oh, Ollie, you're amazing! You saved me from drowning in Big

Water. You're walking me home. And you know your way around Big Woods. I hope we can always be friends." He hoped he could visit his new friends again soon.

The dog stopped and turned to the young raccoon. "Rascal, today you learned how important it is to think ahead before you decide, right?"

"Oh, yes. I'll remember this day and this lesson forever!"

"Well, then, you've earned this green bandana!" Ollie pulled an extra bandana from under his collar and gave it to the young raccoon. "Wear this and be one of the bandana buddies. We're a special group of animals who promise to take care of each other whenever we can. Does that sound good?" Rascal happily accepted and tied it around his neck. "Now that you've learned more directions in Big Woods, you can come back and see us anytime."

Tears puddled in Rascal's eyes. He knew

he'd be friends with this dog forever. "Thank you, Ollie." He touched the edge of the green bandana and felt something he had never felt before. He felt the ties between close friends.

Soon, they heard a noise in the thicket. **BAM!** There was Jasper! "Hi! I knew I could catch up with you two." He stopped to catch his breath from running so fast and long.

Ollie smiled. "I knew you'd make it, Jasper. Guess what? Rascal's a bandana buddy now!"

"Awesome!" Jasper replied. "Welcome to the club, kid."

The three animals finally reached the grove with Rascal's hollow-tree. "Hey! This is it!" He sped up. "Mom!" he shouted. "Mom!"

His mom watched him run toward her. She opened her arms wide. "Oh, Rascal!" She gave him a HUGE hug as he crashed into her. "I was so worried! Oh, I'm glad you're finally home!" She looked over at the dog and rabbit who joined the happy reunion. "Jasper? Ollie?" she asked.

"Mom, these are my friends, Jasper and Ollie. Wait! You know them? After the storm, I was lost. I stayed at Jasper's house. He gave me food in the morning. Then he ran to find Ollie to help me get home. Because my leg was hurt in the storm, I couldn't swim in Big Water. Ollie saved me! Then he showed me the way here." He turned toward them.

"Oh, thank you," she said softly, her eyes meeting theirs. "I remember you both. Thanks for helping my boy." She gave each of them a hug too.

Worn out from the long trip, Ollie and Jasper rested and listened as Rascal shared his adventures with his mom. The little raccoon knew someday, soon, he would visit his new friends again. But next time he'd make wiser choices.

What If?

Things to Think About

In the story:

1. What if Rascal went home before the storm hit?

2. What if Rascal couldn't find a place to hide?

3. What if Jasper wasn't there?

4. What if Jasper & Ollie couldn't find Rascal in Big Water?

In real life, what might happen if...

1. I don't do my homework?

2. I practice a little on my (sport or instrument) every day?

3. I get mad and hit my brother or sister?

4. Someone forgot their lunch and I shared some of mine?

Glossary

Ached had a dull, long-lasting pain

Afloat to stay on top of the water

Bandana colorful, patterned handkerchief

Bounded made a long jump

Brush small bushes or trees

Canopy the highest layer of branches on a tree or in a forest

Coyotes small wild animals related to dog – bigger than fox

Crayfish small fresh-water animal similar to lobster

Dazed not being able to act normally due to injury or surprise

Decided made a choice

Disappear to stop being visible, to go out of sight

Distance the amount of space between things

Eagles large birds who fly high, have great eyesight, and eat animals,birds, and fish

Eased to move slowly and carefully

Excitement high interest and energy level, enthusiasm

Fierce wild, forceful, aggressive

Flashed to appear or pass very suddenly

Footing the ability of your feet to stay where you put them

Grove a small group of trees

Hawks large birds who eat small animals, birds, and fish. Smaller than an eagles

Hobbled walked with difficulty due to injury or weakness

Hovered to float in the air without moving in any direction

Invaded to go into a place without permission, invitation or being wanted

Jiffy quickly, a very brief time, a moment, an instant

Ominous looking like something bad will happen in the future

Panicky not acting or thinking normally because of extreme fear

Peered looking carefully as if at something hard to see clearly

Poked stuck out so that part can be seen

Ravine a small, deep, narrow valley

Ridge a long area of land on top of a hill or mountain

Saucers round and open, like small flat dishes that you put cups on

Scurried moved quickly with short steps, hurried

Shallows the shallow (not deep) part of the water near the land

Sipped drank small amounts of liquid (nectar) into its mouth

Sprinted ran very fast – for a short distance

Squinting to look at something with your eyes partly closed

Surface the top of the water

Surroundings the place, things, conditions around him

Swirled moved in a circular way, curved around

Tadpole small animal that lives in fresh water, has a long tail, and grows up to be a frog or toad

Thicket a group of small bushes or trees that grow close together

Wafted moved lightly through the air

Whirlwind a very strong swirling or spinning, damaging wind

Whisked moved something away very quickly

Whistled moved by or passed with a high pitched sound

Wolverine a very strong member of the weasel family

Yawned opened her mouth while taking a
breath as she was tired

About the Author/Illustrator

Kathy J Perry

BS Elementary Education

A semi-retired elementary school teacher, Kathy now enjoys writing and illustrating early chapter books about animals who learn valuable character qualities. Her goal is to help kids enjoy learning to read as well as apply lessons learned from the animals to their own lives. Her fun, animal adventures will appeal to first and second graders and as read-aloud books to pre-schoolers. Soft, watercolor illustrations have been a source of joy for Kathy to draw and paint. She has a keen interest in art and has designed and created architectural stained glass windows for 35 years for homes and businesses.

About the Character Designer

Mark Baral

Mark Baral, a children's book illustrator and character designer, is currently pursuing his Bachelor's in Studio Art at Pensacola Christian College. Mark has fostered his love for art by consistently drawing and painting, which has enabled him to produce award-winning artwork both at the regional and national level. The process of bringing characters to life through design and illustration has always captured his attention. His love for stories is a great inspiration to him as he strives to create fun and entertaining characters that enhance the storytelling experience. Mark can be contacted at mdbaralkc@gmail.com.

"Owww! Oh, Feebs, I'm trapped! Can you get help?"

Feebs the kitten is new to the farm. She's a long way from the farmhouse and doesn't know her way home in the dark. Her new friend, Ollie the dog, needs help. Can she find the courage to lead a night rescue?

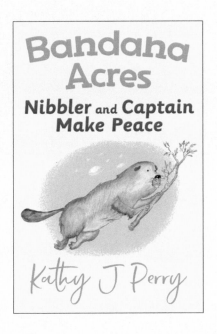

Bandana Acres

Nibbler and **Captain Make Peace**

Kathy J Perry

"This makes me mad! What should I do?"

Nibbler the beaver works hard to keep his lodge and dam perfectly patched. A river otter knocks a hole in his great work. Now he's so angry, he could almost spit nails. Can he learn how to handle his anger?

CHICKADEE
WORDS

"Wait! That's not a coyote.
Is he here to help me?"

FIRE! Kit must find a new home in the
woods. She is surrounded by wild coyotes.
A bandana buddy comes to her rescue.
Did she earn his friendship?

CHICKADEE
WORDS

Available now!
BandanaAcres.com/book-shop/

Wait, there's more!

Visit BandanaAcres.com/gift/

Be sure to ask your parents before you sign up.

CHICKADEE
WORDS